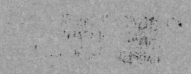

MARIANNA MAYER

Young Mary of Nazareth

MORROW JUNIOR BOOKS

NEW YORK

FOR
Andrea Schneeman
—this book's inspiration—
with gratitude and
deep affection
—MM

The text type is 17-point Jensen.

Published by Morrow Junior Books
a division of William Morrow and Company, Inc.
1350 Avenue of the Americas, New York, NY 10019
www.williammorrow.com

Printed in Singapore at Tien Wah Press.

10 9 8 7 6 5 4 3 2 1

Library of Congress Cataloging-in-Publication Data
Mayer, Marianna.
Young Mary of Nazareth/Marianna Mayer.
p. cm.
Includes bibliographical references.
Summary: An account of the life of the Virgin Mary, from her own birth through
her early years and education at the Temple to the birth of Jesus in Bethlehem.
ISBN 0-688-14061-0 (trade)—ISBN 0-688-14062-9 (library)
1. Mary, Blessed Virgin, Saint—Biography—Juvenile literature.   2. Protevangelium Jacobi—
Biography—Juvenile literature.   3. Mary, Blessed Virgin, Saint—Legends—Juvenile literature.
[1. Mary, Blessed Virgin, Saint.   2. Saints.]   I. Title.   BT607.M35 1998
232.91—dc21   97-38944   CIP AC

N GALILEE LONG AGO, in a town called
Nazareth, there lived a couple named Joachim and Anne. Each year these generous
people divided their wealth into equal portions—one for the Temple, one for the poor,
and one for themselves.

As the day to celebrate the Lord drew near, Joachim went with his offering to the Temple. A priest stood at the door to welcome those who came, but when he saw Joachim, the priest frowned and said, "You must bring your gifts last, for you have no offspring." Deeply ashamed, Joachim left the city. In the desert he pitched a tent, saying, "I shall fast and do penance until the Lord deems me worthy."

Anne wept to see her husband go. All alone, she went into the garden and sat down beneath the laurel tree. Looking toward the heavens, she saw a nest of sparrows in the tree. Fresh tears welled up in her eyes. How she longed to have a child of her own.

When she returned to the house, she saw a dazzling light, and an angel of the Lord stood before her. "Anne, do not be afraid," said the angel. "You shall conceive, and your child shall be called Mary, the exalted one."

At the same time, another angel appeared to Joachim in a dream. "Joachim," said the angel, "return to your wife, for your prayers have been answered."

Joachim hurried home and was met at the city gates by Anne, looking more radiant than ever. As they embraced, Anne whispered to her husband, "The Lord has blessed us, for I shall have a child at last."

Anne gave birth to a beautiful baby girl, and in gratitude to the Lord, Joachim vowed that once the child turned three years old, she would be sent to the Temple to be educated.

Day by day the child grew more lovely. When she was but six months old, her mother stood her on the ground to see if she could stand. And Mary walked seven steps and then, turning, came back to her mother's open arms. Anne held the baby to her and said, "As the Lord is my God, He has sent me a miraculous child."

The months passed, and Mary's first companions were the animals that came to forage in her mother's garden. One evening she returned from the garden carrying something cupped in her small hands. "What do you have there?" asked her mother.

"It is a sparrow with a broken wing," answered Mary. "I have made a tiny splint for it." And indeed, under the child's care the bird was soon able to fly again.

The day Mary set the bird free, Anne embraced her and said, "How well you have done."

"I could not have done as much if I had not had help," explained the little girl.

"Who helped you, child?" asked Anne.

"I prayed for the little bird, and then I knew what must be done."

"The Lord and His messengers must be very close to you," said Anne, remembering the day the angel told her that she would give birth.

On Mary's third birthday, as promised, she was presented to the Temple. That day there was a great feast, and the whole community was invited.

During the celebration, Zaccharia, the chief priest who would oversee Mary's education, was discussing the Scriptures with a small group of holy men. The child sat beside him, for already she was a great favorite with these revered elders.

"The Lord made us to serve Him," Zaccharia declared.

"And to glory in His kindness," said Mary softly.

Startled, the old priest looked at her. "The little one is fearless and yet all gentleness," he told himself as the others exchanged smiles.

"The Lord can be merciful. That is true, Mary," he replied. "You are wise, for one so young."

"Is it wisdom, good father, to see what is all around us?" asked the child. "The Lord must love us very much to have given us this earthly paradise to look after."

At last it was time for Mary to climb the steps to the Temple. A halo of light encircled the blessed child, and, filled with joy, she began to dance. The child's bright spirit could not be contained any more than the sun can be kept from rising. Solemn as he was, the old priest had to smile, as did all those looking on.

But later he took Joachim aside and said, "She is a puzzle, your Mary—strong without being willful, determined without being stubborn. It is good that we begin to educate her early—but perhaps, with such a strong spirit, it will be Mary who educates us." Indeed, the strength of her character would be demonstrated time and again as she grew up in the Temple.

Among Mary's many chores was tapestry making. Anne had taught her well, and the child's talent surpassed the older girls'. When her chores were done, in the remaining hours of each day she went out alone just beyond the gates of the Temple. There she would distribute food and clothing to the poor and the elderly who came hoping for charity. In time the other girls followed her example, and the Temple became known far and wide for its generosity.

One day, as she bathed the brow of a young girl so sick with fever that she was not expected to survive the night, Mary heard angelic singing. She looked to her patient, wondering if the girl had heard it too. No, her friend was sleeping peacefully for the first time in days. Touching the girl's forehead, Mary realized that the fever had passed. Surely it was a miracle—the girl would recover, just as Mary had prayed she would.

"Mary," a voice suddenly said. "The Lord has seen fit to bring you into this world without the stain of sin. And you use His good favor to help others. By doing so you honor Him greatly."

When Mary turned fourteen, Zaccharia told her, "It is customary for all young maidens at your age to marry."

But Mary was uncertain. "My work with the poor and the sick takes so much of my time," she confided. "Perhaps marriage is not for me."

Some days later, Zaccharia returned to the subject, suggesting that she should at least consider the suitors that might come forward to offer themselves. "In this way," the priest advised, "you can make up your own mind on this matter."

Mary agreed, and with her permission, Zaccharia called upon all the eligible suitors. Young bachelors and old widowers flocked to the Temple on the appointed day.

Zaccharia hoped that a widower might be chosen for Mary. An older man, he reasoned, would best appreciate her strong spirit. But which one, he wondered, for there were so many. That night an angel appeared to the old priest in a dream and said, "Do not worry, Zaccharia. Tomorrow, have each suitor bring with him a staff. The Holy Spirit will give a sign as to who shall be Mary's husband."

The next day the suitors crowded into the Temple, each holding a staff in his hand. Kneeling, they prayed for a sign. All at once a lily was seen to bloom from the staff held by the widower Joseph, a builder and carpenter. And then a snow white dove alighted upon the staff before flying off.

"How can it be that the Lord has chosen me?" Joseph said, astonished. "I have been widowed for some time and have sons nearly as old as this tender young girl."

But Zaccharia shook his head. "The Lord has given a sign, Joseph." And turning to Mary, the priest asked, "Mary, what is your wish?"

Moved by the events and Joseph's humble words, Mary extended her hand to Joseph, saying, "I accept."

That day the marriage contract was signed, and in twelve months the wedding ceremony would be celebrated. In the meantime, Mary returned to her parents while Joseph departed for a distant town where he was about to begin work on the building of a Temple. The commission was a great honor, but it would separate the couple for nearly a year.

At daybreak one spring morning, Mary went to draw water from the well before her parents awakened. All at once, she heard a voice. "Hail Mary," it said. "The Lord is with you. Holy is your name."

Suddenly there was a flash of shimmering light, and an angel stood before her. Mary's hands froze and the jug she held fell to the ground, shattering.

The angel picked up the pieces, and when he handed them to Mary, the jug was whole again.

In the next moment the angel vanished, but his words haunted her. Was this what the priests spoke of when describing God's messengers?

That day she tried to go about her chores as usual, saying nothing about the event to anyone. Yet at nightfall Mary could not sleep. Then in the half-light of dawn she heard the angel's voice again.

"Hail Mary. The Lord is with you." And the angel stood before her. "Mary, do not be afraid," he said. "I am the angel Gabriel, God's messenger. He has sent me to tell you that He wishes you to bear a son."

"But how can such a thing be possible? I am not yet wed," said Mary.

"The Holy Spirit will pass through you as a ray of sunlight passes through a drop of water, and so the child will be called the Son of God."

Mary shook her head in wonder.

"Your kinswoman Elizabeth has in her old age conceived a son, and she, like your own mother, was once called barren," the angel continued. "But now, thanks to the Lord, Elizabeth is in her sixth month. Indeed, only your consent is needed for such a miracle to be possible, for nothing is impossible for God."

As she listened, Mary was filled with courage. She replied, "Then I give my consent."

Bowing before her, the angel Gabriel kissed the hem of Mary's robe and then vanished.

Alone, Mary wondered what kind of destiny she had carved for herself. How was she to explain this to her parents? And to Joseph?

The next morning Anne surprised Mary with news. "I have just received a letter from our cousin Elizabeth. The Lord has blessed her, for at last she has conceived a child. It is truly a miracle!"

The following day they left for Elizabeth's home to help her as she awaited the birth of the baby. Now, as soon as Elizabeth heard Mary at the door, she called out, "Hail Mary. Mother of God!" And at the same moment, the infant Elizabeth carried leapt for joy within her.

Rushing to embrace them both, Elizabeth said to Anne, "Of all the women, Mary is the most blessed, and blessed is the infant she carries."

When Mary was alone with her mother, she tried to explain. Anne took her daughter into her arms. "My dearest child, I believe you," said Anne. "But what of Joseph? Will he trust in you as completely?"

When Joseph was told, he blamed himself, for he felt he had failed to protect her. To spare Mary any public shame, it was decided that she was to go into seclusion, and that the engagement would be broken. But that very night an angel appeared to Joseph in a dream and said, "Joseph, do not be afraid to take Mary as your wife. She has conceived her child through the grace of the Holy Spirit. It will be a son, and you must name him Jesus, for he will be the salvation of the world."

The following day Joseph and Mary went to the Temple. Explaining the situation to Zaccharia, they asked that the wedding ceremony be performed at once. But the priest said, "So that there should not be a breath of scandal surrounding your union, will you agree to undergo a test of truth by drinking the sacred waters of conviction? Be warned: If all you say is true, the water will do you no harm—but if you lie, it will result in death."

Holding tight to each other's hands, Mary and Joseph drank the sacred water. When moments passed and no harm came to either, Zaccharia said, "Today these two people shall be joined in marriage, and let no one doubt that the Lord is with them."

When Mary was near the time to give birth, a census was announced. To comply, Joseph had to register in the little town of Bethlehem, where his family still resided. It was a few days' journey, and not wishing to be separated, the couple set out together.

Along the outskirts of the town, Joseph became concerned for his wife. Pale and in pain, Mary said they should go no farther, for the baby would soon be delivered. Immediately Joseph began knocking on every door they passed, looking for a place to stay, but there was no room. At last an innkeeper took pity on them. "My inn is full," said the man, "but you are welcome to stay in my stable."

Joseph settled Mary in the stable and then went to find them food. When he was gone, the farm animals huddled around the expectant mother. The scent of fresh hay and animals brought a smile to young Mary's lips. "As you have been my friends ever since I was a small child," said Mary, stroking each of them, "I am glad that I will give birth to my son among you."

PARVVLVS NAT̄ Ē NOB̄ 7 FILI̅ DAT̄ Ē NOBIS 7 FACT̄ Ē PRINCIPAT̄ SVP HVMERV̄ EI̅. YSA. IX. C.

And so it was that in this humble shelter the infant Jesus was born.
The animals' sweet breath fell fondly upon the baby infant as he came
forth into the world. And their warmth comforted them both—
Mary, the Mother of God, and her Son,
who would one day be called
the Light of the
World.

A Note about This Book

This portrait of the Virgin Mary's girlhood is a very personal interpretation. In part, the details of Mary's birth and childhood are based on the scant material documented in the Gospels according to James, Luke, and Matthew. Further material, such as the story of the "waters of conviction," can be found in the writings of the early saints and mystics. To more fully illustrate Mary's character, certain incidents were drawn from my imagination as well as from my vivid memories of the Apocryphal tales passed on by the nuns of Saint Joseph in the convent school where my early education took place. Mary's relationships with her mother and the priest Zaccharia, her healing of the bird and the sick girl, as well as her good works at the Temple—all emphasize Mary's courage. Indeed, it was Mary's strength of character as much as her goodness that caused her to *choose* to do the will of God.

Most revered of all saints, perhaps rivaling even Christ as a focus of personal devotion, the Blessed Virgin embodies the very essence of the powerful pagan Great Mother goddesses that went before her. Her presence in the Roman Catholic Church then and now has elevated womanhood to the level of the sacred, replacing darker examples, such as Lilith and Eve, with a woman heretofore unparalleled in biblical scripture.

Acknowledgments

No book of this kind can be done without assistance from a variety of knowledgeable individuals. Many thanks, then, must go to the following: Marie Pontois, another convent school veteran and friend, for her inspiration and translation of certain materials from French to English at the early stages of this project; Rev. Johann G. Roten, S.M., chairman of the International Marian Institute at the University of Dayton, Ohio, an invaluable source for a wealth of Marian material; and Stephanie Leone, for her assistance in the unearthing of just the right paintings for this book. Last but not least, many thanks to my editor, Andrea Schneeman, whose idea it was to undertake the project, and who followed through with creative input at every stage.

Sources

Brown, Raphael, ed. *The Life of Mary—As Seen by Mystics*. Rockford, Ill.: Tan Books, 1951.

Eicher, Peter. *Vision of Mary*. New York: Avon, 1996.

Emmerich, Anne Catherine. *The Life of the Blessed Virgin Mary*, trans. by Sir Michael Palairet. London: Burns & Oates, 1954.

Mary of Agreda. *The City of God—The Divine History and Life of the Virgin Mary* in four volumes: *Conception, Incarnation, Transfixion, Coronation*, trans. by Fiscar Marison. Washington, N.J.: Ami Press, 1996.

Pelikan, Jaroslaw. *Mary Through the Centuries—Her Place in the History of Culture*. New Haven, Conn.: Yale University Press, 1996.

Warner, Marina. *Alone of All Her Sex*. New York: Vintage, 1983.

List of Illustrations